FOCUS

Copyright © [2024]

Disclaimer

This Book has been written for information purposes only. Every effort has been made to make this Book as complete and accurate as possible. However, there may be mistakes in typography or content. Also, this Book provides information only up to the publishing date. Therefore, this eBook should be used as a guide - not as the ultimate source.

The purpose of this Book is to educate. The author and the publisher do not warrant that the information contained in this Book is fully complete and shall not be responsible for any errors or omissions. The author and publisher shall have neither liability nor responsibility to any person or entity with respect to any loss or damage caused or alleged to be caused directly or indirectly by this book.

This Book offers information and is designed for educational purposes only. You should not rely on this information as a substitute for, nor does it replace professional medical advice, diagnosis, or treatment.

Table of Content

Introduction

Introduction

In the bustling heart of the city, there lived a young woman named Light. She had big dreams and aspirations, but no matter how hard she tried, she always found herself getting distracted by the constant buzz of social media. Every time she set out to achieve her goals, she would inevitably find herself scrolling through her feeds, losing precious hours to mindless browsing.

Light's lack of focus began to take its toll on her life. She missed deadlines at work, her relationships suffered, and worst of all, she felt like she was constantly falling short of her own potential. Frustrated and disillusioned, she began to wonder if she would ever be able to break free from the cycle of distraction and achieve the success she so desperately desired.

One day, while browsing through a local bookstore, Light stumbled upon a book titled "Unlock Your Focus: Intrigued, she decided to give it a chance. As she delved into its pages, she discovered a wealth of practical tips and techniques for overcoming distractions, boosting productivity, and harnessing the power of her mind.

With newfound determination, Light began to implement the strategies outlined in the book. She started setting specific goals, creating a distraction-free workspace, and practicing mindfulness to quiet her racing thoughts. Slowly but surely, she began to notice a profound shift in her ability to concentrate and stay on task.

Weeks turned into months, and Light found herself making significant progress towards her goals. She landed a promotion at work, rekindled her relationships with friends and family, and even found the time to pursue her passions outside of her career. Her life transformed from one of constant distraction and disappointment to one of focus, fulfillment, and success. And it was all thanks to the wisdom she found within the pages of that book.

So, if you find yourself struggling to stay focused amidst the chaos of modern life, remember Emily's story. With the right guidance and determination, you too can unlock your full potential and achieve the success you've always dreamed of by following the steps in this book, I can assure you that you will see amazing result in your life exactly like light or even more.

I t might be difficult to stay focused in a world full with distractions and noise. Our attention is being drawn in so many different directions that it is nearly hard to concentrate on the things that are actually important. There are constantly things that can divert our focus from finishing our task, including social media, text messages, phone calls, and even in-person visits.

We consequently get a sense of being behind. There is less time left over to complete projects and other work when we spend the most of the day reading through pointless emails or checking Facebook notifications. We may become overworked and feel as though we are not making any progress as a result of this, leaving us feeling overwhelmed.

This handbook aims to rectify all of that. To avoid having to remain late at work to finish projects or wasting time away from our loved ones, the objective is to learn how to focus our attention and manage our time. Within, we'll discover that we truly have power over our time—not the clock—and that we can accomplish our goals on the timetable of our own choosing.

We will discover the value of goal-setting, avoiding distractions, and even taking breaks as we move through this manual. We have access to some of the greatest concentration techniques.

We can do more by using time management strategies like Eat the Frog and the Pomodoro Method. By gradually incorporating a few of these suggestions one at a time, you can begin to form these concepts into routines and sharpen your concentration when doing tasks.

Give up allowing the world's noise and distractions to overcome you. Give up feeling like nothing gets done and becoming a slave to the clock. Examine this manual to determine the precise actions you may do to get back your concentration and time!

The Psychology of
Staying Focused

Chapter 1: The Psychology of Staying Focused

The amount of items competing for our attention at the moment seems never-ending. It's nearly hard to keep up with everything—our phones, emails, family, and a lengthy to-do list, among other things. Even though contemporary technology is incredible and has greatly improved our world, it has the unintended consequence of always capturing our attention.

Consider your phone. One notification after another frequently appears, diverting our attention from the tasks at hand. Suddenly, we've spent an hour and still have a ton of work to accomplish. It is hard to advance when this keeps happening throughout the day.

In this issue, you are not by yourself. Every three minutes, the typical office worker will come across a distraction. Furthermore, research from Carnegie Mellon University's Human-Computer Interaction Institute indicates that it can take up to 25 minutes to refocus after being distracted. In conclusion, it is simple to lose attention and difficult to regain it. We could be more concerned with too many distractions than an excess of effort.

How the Brain Selects Items to Focus On?

Your brain is always working throughout the day to process and assimilate crucial information. It must therefore choose what to focus on by filtering out background noise. Selective attention is what this is known as, and it comes in two primary forms:

Top-Down

This is among the best and is often referred to as voluntary focus. You are aware of your objectives when you have this focus. After taking a broad view, you devise a strategy that gets you there.

You ignore your phone and emails since you know they will prevent you from achieving your objectives. You complete tasks on schedule, if not ahead of schedule.

Bottom-Up

This concentration is more stimulus-driven. You are using bottom-up focus when an idea begins to seep into your mind or when you become sidetracked when a notification appears on your phone. Instead of focusing on what you think needs the greatest attention, you need to pay attention to what is going on around you.

What is the issue at hand?

The end game is to learn how to think from the top down. This enables us to ignore everything else and concentrate on what matters. Regretfully, we tend to focus from the bottom up due to our innate tendencies. Since willpower and concentration are limited resources, it becomes more difficult to get back on course the more sidetracked you become. Furthermore, because we are bottom-up focusers, anything might derail us from our objectives.

We should be ready for this because the majority of us are easily sidetracked by small things like emails and phone notifications. We must be conscious of this and minimize the number of outside distractions we encounter throughout the day. For example, turning off your phone and avoiding social media might help reduce distractions so your brain won't even know they're there and you can concentrate on your work.

There is simply too much trying to divert our attention from what is crucial and exacerbate our focus issue. Even if they are not particularly significant, those emails, notifications, and other small things have a way of grabbing our attention. We believe we just give them brief periods of our time, but it doesn't take long for them to gain control, at which point we are unable to complete any tasks during the day.

Calls and Notifications Are Equally Distracting

Previously, we would be unaware that someone was attempting to reach us on our phones until they rang. This was less common because phone conversations took time, so most individuals needed to have something significant to talk about before making the effort. Our phones don't ring as much these days. However, we might hear a single beep or vibration in response to a Facebook message or SMS. We might receive a large number of them throughout the day because they just take a few minutes to send.

According to a study conducted by three Florida State University researchers, receiving one of these notifications—regardless of how little—may divert our attention just as much as answering a call or sending a text message, even if we choose not to reply.

About 150 pupils were required to finish a sustained attentional performance test as part of this investigation. A sequence of single digits is presented to the test subjects on a screen; a new digit will appear every second.

The pupils are supposed to tap the keyboard whenever a digit changes during this, unless it's a 3. Every individual completed the exam twice. They accomplished it without their gadgets there to distract them the first time. On the second attempt, they might have their phones with them, and test assistants could text or call these phones.

Through this, researchers discovered that if a student received any kind of auditory notification on their phone, it negatively impacted their performance on the evaluation. Whether it was a text or a call, any kind of phone distraction was detrimental to their performance. If the student disregarded the text or didn't answer the phone, it didn't appear to matter. If they received the notification, they were still aware of it, and as a result, their performance declined.

This demonstrates bottom-up thinking in action and serves as a cue for our attention. As little as a text notification has the power to divert our attention and impair our performance. If you want to perform better at work, you may need to acknowledge this and figure out ways to reduce the effect it has on our work.

Find
Your Willpower

Chapter 2: Find Your Willpower

There are things you can do to lessen the impact of your bottom-up attention and easy distraction tendency. There are things you can do if you're sick of letting social media or your phone notifications eat up your time and you don't want to put in extra hours to finish the work. Finding your motivation and your willpower can help, even though it won't always be simple.

We need to look at how to discover your willpower before we get into some of the mechanics of managing your attention. This can be achieved by grasping the Pareto Principle and developing the ability to define specific objectives for oneself.

The Pareto Principle

According to the Pareto Principle, 20% of the causes of any given scenario will account for 80% of the results. This demonstrates that the inputs and outputs have an uneven connection. It is frequently known as the 80/20 rule.

Although the initial application of this theory concerned the population-wealth relationship, it can also be extended to a wide range of other domains, such as manufacturing, human resources, and management. It can also be used in a more private context. One common application of the Pareto Principle is in time management.

Instead of concentrating on the things that are most crucial, a lot of people have a tendency to fragment their time. In this instance, 20% of your working hours may produce 80% of your output connected to your job.

Establishing and Setting Goals

Setting goals will enable you to make the most of your workday. This gives you something more to strive toward and improves your ability to stay focused. Get more done shouldn't be your aim. If you want to see results, it needs to be more targeted and concentrated.

Having a goal is the greatest approach to set one. SMART Goal. These represent specific, measurable, attainable, relevant, and time-bound.

These might provide you with the details you require to achieve your aspirations and advance. They may also serve as a source of inspiration to keep going rather than quitting up midway through.

You can base your goal-setting on what is most effective for you. Would you like to set yourself the objective of not becoming sidetracked at work? Next, establish a goal for the amount of time you will allow yourself to spend checking emails and phone calls. Employ the SMART Goals concept to help you stay on track if you are working on a large project at work.

Let's imagine you frequently finish tasks at the last minute and you have a significant project at work that needs to be completed. This moment, we're going to employ SMART GOALS. Make a list of everything you intend to accomplish for the goals. We intend to finish the project entirely by the deadline for this one.

Then, we will divide it into more doable and quantifiable components, assigning a realistic deadline to each component. The precise project you need to complete will determine how you divide things up, but breaking it up into smaller, more manageable pieces can make life easier and give you something to cross off as you go. Many people may find motivation in this along.

Never forget to provide a deadline to every objective you hope to accomplish. Making a list of the things you want to get done and then leaving them undone is simple. Due to your tendency to put things off, this is the quickest route to trouble. To avoid having to put off doing the work until the last minute, set a goal and stick to it with a time limit that makes sense for that portion of the project.

You may make the most of the Pareto Principle by creating goals. It's remarkable how quickly you can finish tasks and move on to something more essential when you are well-organized and able to stay on task. You have specific goals that will help you achieve, so stop wasting time at work or at home and stop waiting until the last minute to complete tasks.

Don't worry about how to get yourself organized and set your SMART GOALS. I will leave a journal space at the end of the book to jot down your ideas and start with your Goals setting. Thanks to me, right!

Create a Focus
Haven

Chapter 3: Create a Focus Haven

It is simpler to ignore your task in favor of looking at the distractions around you the more of them there are. When your brain detects a ding, a missed message, or an email, it automatically assumes the information is critical and must be responded to immediately. Naturally, this isn't always the case and is merely a simple diversion.

Establishing a focus refuge surrounding your workspace is essential if you want to increase your ability to concentrate. Turn off any distractions, including noise, that frequently get in the way. Uncertain about those sources of distraction? For a few days, observe what things or noises tend to divert your attention from your task when you should be working.

Your productivity can significantly increase in a space free of all those distractions. You won't believe how much more you can get done during the day when your phone doesn't beep or vibrate all the time. Without tension, you might even be able to finish the assignment early!

You can establish your focal refuge in a number of ways, such as:

Switch Off Email and Social Media

Turning off the emails and social media is the first step towards creating your focus hideaway. One of the largest time wasters available is social media, which won't enable you to do any necessary tasks. Simply switch it off as soon as you're ready to start your task. If necessary, configure your emails to notify senders that you are occupied and will get back to them at a later time. In an emergency, they can always come knocking on your door.

Switch Off Your Phone

Our phones are always bombarding us with information and potentially distracting items because they are connected to so many different things.

Our phones ring constantly from texts, calls, emails, and social media alerts. It's advisable to switch off your phone when working if at all feasible. After you've caught up, you can check some of the crucial emails and other sections by turning the phone back on.

Use some creativity if your employment requires you to answer the phone while working. Set it up such that it will only ring or send a message to someone significant and not to do so in response to any other messages.

Shut the Door

There are a lot of distractions that you invite inside when you leave your door open. It doesn't take long to notice anything that distracts you from your work because you can clearly hear all the noise and other activity that occurs in neighboring offices and down the corridor. Furthermore, there's always the possibility that someone will see the open door and come say hello. A brief inquiry can quickly develop into an all-consuming socialization session.

Close the door to the office when you have work to do. Try to give the impression that you are not even there. A closed door reduces the cacophony of sounds surrounding you in the office and decreases the likelihood that someone will knock on it to speak. You'll be able to accomplish a lot of your work with this.

Play Some Classical Music

The greatest music for this is classical. It's something that, without being a distraction in and of itself, can help fill in the voids left by quiet or muffle distracting sounds. Refrain from including any of your own music. Even while listening to your favorite band can be enjoyable, you won't be able to sing along to your favorite song for very long. Plus, studies have shown that listening to classical music can enhance focus! In order to minimize distractions during work, play some classical music in the background.

Organize

To help with this one, you might need to put some thought into your planning. Maintaining organization can help you avoid becoming sidetracked and avoid having to look all over the place for the items you need. A project can take a long time to complete and slow you down if you have to pause and ask someone for help or look for the supplies you need.

Having everything in its proper place and keeping things organized will have a significant impact on your productivity. Additionally, it removes the possibility that you will divert your attention from your work when working. Every object will be readily available to you, and all you have to do is reach for it.

There are several approaches you can take to this one. Spend some time first organizing your entire workspace. Arrange things that you use frequently together in close proximity to one another. Store things away and discard anything that becomes in the way or is garbage that you are no longer using. Then, while you're trying to make your to-do list at night, gather the supplies you'll need and arrange them in one place for every task you want to finish. Then, you won't have to look around as much because you can just grab the objects and use them as needed.

You can reduce distractions and maintain focus at work when you can create a more peaceful and distraction-free environment for yourself while you're working. You will discover that it is simpler to unwind and concentrate if you turn off the phone and email and make it more difficult for people to find you so they won't stop by.

To have a more organized life, either at home, office, work place, or anywhere, CHECK THIS BOOK OUT. I have dwell so much on it and I hope it will change your life as it has help people who used the tips and tricks in the book

Staying Focused
in a Digital Age

Chapter 4: Staying Focused in the Digital Age

Our ability to focus has suffered due to the digital age. When a little notification appears on Facebook or an email or text message appears on their phone, even the most driven individuals can become easily sidetracked. It could be challenging to maintain concentrate and complete any tasks as a result. It will only get worse as new technology is developed on a constant basis.

The Distraction Caused by Our Phones

Our biggest distractions are frequently our phones. These days, they are more than simply a basic phone. They provide us phone calls, texts, emails, and social media alerts all in one. It is understandable that they will give us hours of amusement and diversion, making it nearly difficult for us to do our work.

It will be challenging to focus when our phones are constantly beeping. We immediately want to pay attention when we hear the ding or vibration on our phones, informing us that we have a text, email, or other alert. Even when we acknowledge that the information is probably not that significant and can wait, we will still be bothered by it until we check because our attention has been diverted. It takes time away from work and can make it difficult to return to it, particularly if it occurs frequently.

Even though they are incredibly helpful tools, phones are among the biggest sources of distraction when trying to complete tasks. Eliminating your phone should be your first priority if you're serious about improving your focus. To prevent all of these distractions and stay focused, you might need to give your phone to someone else or turn it off.

You have to become a digital minimalist, at least while you're trying to finish your task. This essentially indicates that technology must be replaced if it is not required to complete the task. Turn everything off if you can complete the task without using any technology at all. Your objective is to see how much of the technology you can switch off or remove from the area, then time how quickly you can return your attention to it.

Perhaps you have a project report that has to be completed. Take around 30 minutes to search for the information you require on the internet, print down emails containing pertinent details, and compile all the material you require. Once you've spent thirty minutes printing everything, shut off the internet. Once you have completed writing the report, shut off the entire computer. Go ahead and physically turn off the Wi-Fi while working if you must type it up.

This is a crucial matter. Don't think that using a computer to browse social media, conduct internet searches, check emails, or do anything else will keep you from doing these things. Some may be able to accomplish this without having to turn off everything else. Others might feel pressured to constantly check items. The only program you can use while the Wi-Fi is unplugged is Word or other comparable program that doesn't require a data connection.

Remember to switch off the other electronic devices in your business. Switch off all devices that could link you to the internet and the outside world from your office, including the phone and speakers. That can wait; you don't have time for it right now.

You have no more distractions now that everything has been switched off. The previous research you found can be used to assist you create your report and complete tasks. Do not pick up your phone or switch the internet back on if you have a query or need to double check something. Put a brief note on a post-it note and refer to it once all the job is finished. When you put all of your attention toward finishing a report instead of focusing on all of the distractions around you, you'll be astounded at how quickly it may be completed.

Every case of digital minimalism is going to be a little bit different. If you are an expert in social media, you will most likely need to be on Facebook or a comparable platform in order to do the assignment. However, you can silence your phone and email during that period and ensure that you exclusively use work-related social media accounts—not personal ones. Consider how many digital devices you can turn off before starting each job you work on, and observe the impact.

You're In Control
of Your Time

Chapter 5: The Power to Manage Your Time

The fact that they are in charge of their time is something that a lot of people overlook. When projects have last-minute deadlines, they feel overburdened because they believe there simply aren't enough hours in the day to finish everything. However, you can simply learn how to take charge of your time and complete tasks on time if you put in the necessary amount of effort and use effective time management skills.

Parkinson's Law

The theory known as Parkinson's Law states that work grows to fill the amount of time available to complete it. This essentially indicates that the time you give yourself to do a task is the exact amount of time needed to achieve it. Thus, if you have three weeks to prepare an essay, you will need to use that entire time to finish it. You will finish the assignment in a week if you give yourself that much time.

The general notion is that you can do the work in the required amount of time, while there are certain exceptions (you can't write a 100-word document in an hour). For this reason, even if you had three weeks to prepare an essay, you could still finish it in time if you had just one week.

It will take you that much longer to complete the task if you set the deadline or the objective too far away. No matter how far in advance you set your deadline, it will still take that long to complete. Establish the deadline earlier if you want to ensure that your task is completed on time rather than at the last minute. Set a goal for yourself to do it in a week, even if the deadline is three weeks away, and see the impact. You might be shocked at how fast you can finish that project!

The Pomodoro Method

If you find it difficult to maintain your focus on a work, you can consider using the Pomodoro Technique. This strategy can help you stay focused and complete tasks if you find that little distractions get in the way, you frequently have to work past the point at which you are most productive, or you have open-ended work that could take an indefinite period of time, like studying for an exam.

The primary concept is to schedule little periods of time during which you will do tasks. You start working and try to get as much done as you can in the allotted time with the aid of a timer. You take a rest after the timer goes off. This may help you be more concentrated and get more done since it lets you know that you have little periods of time when you can really focus, followed by a break.

This method's main component is working in 25-minute sprints. If required and if they are short, you can combine a few smaller tasks within the same sprint. Once a job is completed, move on to the following item on your to-do list. Never finish in the allotted 25 minutes before getting sidetracked and checking your emails. While the timer is running, you need to finish your work; you can do that later.

This method is easy to use. It permits working hours as well as well-timed pauses for self-care. To use this technique:

- Acquire a timer and a to-do list. Make a list of everything you need to do and prioritize the things that are most important.

- After setting a 25-minute timer, concentrate on just one task until the alarm goes off. It can take several of these 25-minute sprints to finish certain larger chores, but the idea is to focus on one thing at a time. Put any minor projects you have together and complete them in a single sprint.

- After finishing the session, cross off one pomodoro and make a note of what was accomplished.
- When that's over, take a brief pause to stretch and walk around.
- It's time for a break when four of these cycles are finished. After all that effort, give yourself 15 to 30 minutes to relax and walk around!
- You'll discover that you are able to accomplish far more with these brief but strong periods of concentration and attention. Although this brief window of time doesn't seem like much, it can pile up rapidly and allow you to go forward with your task.

As you proceed, be sure to keep in mind to take those pauses. It is simple to desire to work nonstop and put in a lot of hours. And it's great that you desire to finish the task. Maybe you could even do a couple of these sprints without stopping. However, the goal of this technique is to assist you in engaging in severe concentration, therefore your brain will require a break. After several hours of intense effort, even thirty minutes can have a significant impact.

Eat the frog.

Eat the Frog is another strategy you can use to make sure you do all of the things you have to get done during the day. The plan is to tackle the most critical assignment first thing in the morning and finish it as soon as possible. If eating a frog is part of your morning job, then you should do it early to avoid having to think about it all day. Eat the largest frog first if you have to eat two frogs or have two important tasks to complete during the day.

It is not the intention to do this assignment and call it a day afterward. However, concentrating on the one major activity at hand can assist clear your mind. Since you prioritize that task first, you are not distracted by the large project all day. After it's finished, you will have a lot of spare time to devote to other activities. Furthermore, doing the major task first makes the other tasks appear simpler and quicker to complete.

In order to apply the Eat the Frog technique, you will:

- Determine which frog you are: This will be the hardest or most significant task of the day.
- Eat it: This denotes that you start working and finish the assignment straight away. Don't put it off or attempt to complete it later.
- Repeat it: You will locate the frog every day and devour it without delay.

After completing that major assignment, you can get to work on some of the other things you need to get done. However, now that you've completed the major work, you won't have to worry about it looming over you or being put off till the last minute.

Although the name of this method may appear strange, the concept is the same. The hardest or least fun task needs to be completed first thing in the morning. In this sense, it's not observing you throughout the day. While you concentrate on finishing all the other tasks, you might finish it and feel relieved.

Which Is Better: Multitasking or Single Tasking?

You must do one task at a time using each of the above-discussed ways. No matter how many things you have to complete, they all need you to choose one at a time and give it your whole attention until it is finished. After finishing that task, you can go on to the next one, and the one after that, and so forth.

This is because it's usually ideal to handle a single task at a time. Our common misconception is that we are more productive when we multitask. This is incorrect. We frequently become more distracted and find it difficult to focus when we multitask. When we try to do a lot of tasks at once, we also don't finish them very well.

When we single task, we only pay attention to one thing at a time, avoiding any distractions from other tasks that can interfere with our progress. Additionally, by concentrating all of our attention on a single activity until it is completed rather than dividing it between two or more, we are able to perform better on the one task. This frequently helps us finish the assignment more quickly as well.

You may not realize it, but you actually have more influence over your time than you may think when it comes to finishing your task on time. Having a solid comprehension of Parkinson's Law and being aware of some of the various time management strategies available to you, you'll quickly discover that you have far more time in a day than you ever could have anticipated.

Don't Forget
to Take a Break

Chapter 6: Don't Forget to Take a Break

It is simple to become enthused about some of the techniques we covered in the previous chapter and believe you must work quickly to finish everything. However, it's also crucial to make sure you take enough of breaks while using any of these techniques. Our minds are not built to work for hours at a time trying to do everything. Also, pressuring them to do so can wear us out. The distractions will arrive soon enough.

For this reason, all of the techniques we covered above include built-in breaks. After finishing a task, you should take a break. You are meant to take a break after completing one of the Pomodoro Method's sprints, and another, longer one, after completing four. Taking breaks can greatly improve your ability to concentrate and maintain focus.

It will be beneficial to take pauses from any mental labor that you undertake. It can increase your productivity and make it simpler for you to concentrate. The following are a few advantages of including breaks in your day:

Increases Your Productivity

According to recent studies, taking a break of about an hour can increase productivity compared to working continuously without one. After a while, our minds are going to become fatigued from the constant stimulation, which will make it difficult for them to complete the activity or see its importance. Taking a break allows us to return to our work with renewed vigor and increased concentration.

Could Serve as Your Inspiration

You can't remain creative and concentrated when your mind is fatigued, even if you truly enjoy what you do. A little walk around your workplace or a quick drink can help you calm and give your brain a little respite—even for 10 minutes. This can provide you with enough of a break to enable you to approach the issue differently and come up with the ideal solution.

Maintaining Physical Activity Sharpens the Brain

It is a good idea to get up and walk around as much as you can during your break. Try jumping jacks or taking a stroll around the workplace. Try spending a few minutes outside if you are able to. Engaging in physical activity, coupled with exposure to sunlight and fresh air, can effectively eliminate any fatigue that may arise from a demanding workday. While being focused helps you complete tasks, it also strains the brain and can cause it to age more quickly than usual. These beneficial breaks that increase heart rate through exercise may be exactly what you need.

It is simple to slip into the trap of believing that we must spend eight hours a day at our desks, giving our whole concentration and attention to the job at hand. This will quickly tire you out and reduce your ability to concentrate and be productive. While maintaining focus is essential to completing tasks, taking regular breaks also helps prevent brain fatigue while working.

Fuel Up

Chapter 7: Get Powered Up

Taking good care of your body is a crucial component in improving your ability to concentrate. The brain cannot concentrate or function as it should if it is not getting enough sleep or eating the correct foods to give the body the essential nutrients. If one or both of these are not in place, you will find it difficult to complete any tasks during the day. The other strategies can work wonders in helping you stay focused and accomplish more during the day, but they rely on your diet and sleep patterns for support.

How Sleep Improves Focus

It is very simple to put off getting the necessary amount of sleep. Even though you might not think it matters much, staying up late and losing a few hours of sleep might have a negative impact on your quality of sleep. It's beneficial to get adequate sleep since it improves our ability to think effectively, make wise judgments, and retain knowledge.

An insufficient amount of sleep will lead to impairments in executive function. Basically, we use this collection of skills to succeed in our jobs, our studies, and every aspect of our lives. When we sleep, our brains become clear and enables us to concentrate, retain knowledge, and be creative. Lack of sleep makes it impossible for us to accomplish any of this.

When was the last time you slept through the night? You might have worked on a significant assignment or had to stay up late with the kids. You felt exhausted and found it difficult to accomplish anything, despite your best efforts, after only a few hours of sleep. When can this occur, albeit to a lesser extent? Every day, you lose out on several hours of sleep.

It could be time to take a closer look at your sleep routine if you discover that your concentration is simply not where you would like it to be. Having a regular sleep schedule, which is going to bed and waking up at the same time every day, will have a significant impact on your morning mood. Additionally, try to get at least eight hours of sleep. This allows your mind to calm and erase the clutter, allowing you to work with the sharpest focus possible.

Choosing the Correct Diet

Maintaining your focus can be greatly aided by eating a nutritious diet. Foods high in sugar and unhealthy fats might impair cognitive function and make it more difficult to concentrate. Eating the correct foods will help you concentrate on whatever work you have to complete during the day.

The primary food that will assist in controlling your energy and mood is food. When it comes to your attention, these two are crucial. You shouldn't stuff your body with a ton of cookies, chocolate syrup, pop, or other products huge help you run, just as it's not a good idea to put some olive oil in your automobile to make it run.

Food has a truly remarkable power to influence your mood, mental clarity, memory, and concentration. It could be time to examine your diet if you are still having trouble concentrating and finishing tasks during the day.

We may experience a brief spike in energy when we consume sugar-filled foods or drinks. For a short while, we could feel fantastic, yet this enthusiasm is really ephemeral. We experience a significant crash right after the sugar high ends. From there, it is impossible to maintain our necessary level of focus, let alone remain attentive. Good diet helps maintain a stable energy level so we can concentrate all day.

Numerous foods, such as blueberries and green tea, make claims about how they can improve memory and focus. The most crucial thing, though, is to concentrate on eating a generally better diet. For prolonged focus, it may be better to eat foods that nourish the body rather than those that will offer you a brief spike in energy before making the sugar crash difficult to handle.

A nutritious diet rich in fruits, vegetables, and lean proteins is an excellent place to start. Your body will receive all the vitamins and minerals it requires from these to remain sharp. Also, keep some nutritious snack options available throughout the office. You never know when all of your hard work will wear you out, so having something convenient to grab that will fuel your body can help you avoid overindulging in unhealthy food that will divert your attention.

You must concentrate on giving your body the proper nourishment if you want to have the kind of attention that allows you to finish tasks quickly. Getting enough sleep at night and eating foods that help you receive all the vitamins and minerals you need can really help. Hunger pains can be relieved.

Make It a Habit

Chapter 8: Develop a Routine

The actions we discussed above are all excellent ways to help you become more focused. It will be simpler for you to focus and complete more tasks during the day if you set specific goals for yourself, follow through on them, get enough rest and nutrition, and use basic time management strategies.

However, things won't always be simple. There will be moments when you'd rather to use your phone than complete the task at hand. For the first few days after experimenting with these various methods, you could find that you are able to accomplish more work. However, after a few days, you might desire to revert to your previous behaviors and not persevere.

It won't be enough to simply go through some of the aforementioned tactics if you want to increase your focus and see results; you also need to make them into daily habits. If you go to bed and wake up at the same hour every day for a month, you will develop a habit that will be more difficult to change. When you develop the habit of Eating the Frog as soon as you arrive at work, it becomes second nature to you.

What is a Habit?

Throughout this process, you want to develop some habits by doing some of the things we covered in this book. Simply put, a habit is a pattern of behavior that we form via repeated exposure. It can frequently be applied to enhance our execution of that pattern. Once we have completed it sufficiently, we won't have to think about it.

You will benefit much from this since it will enable you to accomplish more tasks without having to think about them. Turning off your phone immediately when you walk into your office is a practice that helps you stay focused and avoid distractions while working. Setting up a to-do list and using the

Pomodoro Method to concentrate on sprints allows you to start working without feeling overwhelmed. Take it one habit at a time to begin with. With this book, I hope to have provided you with a ton of helpful tips to help you succeed.

While taking them all on at once is a commendable objective, doing so may overwhelm you and may make it difficult for you to remain focused and on target. Start with one or two that you believe are significant. Perhaps within the first few weeks, you decide you want to try the Pomodoro Method and set an intention to go to bed 30 minutes sooner.

You can notice progress from there, and that might be enough to encourage you to give a couple more techniques a try.

How to Form a Habit?

After receiving all the necessary tools to manage your time effectively and increase your focus, it's time to make using them a daily habit that will allow you to do more.

Among the actions you can do to form new habits are:

- **Concentrate on one habit at a time:** If you use your phone a lot during the day, consider establishing a rule to check it no more than once every hour. After that, you can choose a time management strategy and create a concentration area in your office. One small task at a time makes everything easier to manage and helps you become more focused as you may make all of them second nature. It is not necessary to tackle the most difficult habit at first; instead, start with a smaller one. Begin with a little task.

- **Be clear about your intent:** You must be committed to the end result and be specific. Here, merely trying to accomplish more during the day is insufficient as a goal. Make a detailed plan of action outlining how you will accomplish all of your goals. In the event that you choose to apply the Eat the Frog approach, decide which task you will accomplish the day before and set aside time to work on it in the morning without interruptions.

- **Monitor your progress:** Since the pomodoro technique requires you to record your accomplishments after each short sprint, it may be useful for this. Compare notes after a few weeks of practice to see how much more you are able to achieve. When you train your focus and learn to manage your own time, you might be surprised at how much you can do.

Developing a new habit is not a very difficult procedure. There aren't many steps to follow. The difficult thing is actually carrying all of this out. The most difficult thing about forming a new habit is beginning. It will be simpler to just keep at it if you can get past the challenging phase and complete the task for a few weeks or perhaps a month. At that point, it will become a habit.

IMPROVE YOUR MENTAL FOCUS

Everyone was present. You have a mile-long to-do list. When you sit down to work, your brain refuses to cooperate. Your focus will stray more the harder you try to force it.

For some people, this is merely an occasional issue. For some, it may be a daily struggle that lasts the entire day. There are a lot of diversions in the modern world. There's always something more interesting you might be doing with your day, even if you love what you do. In today's society, the next notification could arrive in a matter of seconds. Your gadgets are clamoring for your attention all the time.

Thus, how do you ignore the blinking lights, cut through the digital clutter, and force your mind to function? All it takes to sharpen your mental attention is "practice makes perfect." Even the most easily distracted mind can break through the clouds and be productive with the right plan and healthy habits

Establish Clear Goals

Finding the thing you need to focus on is the first step. Your thoughts will stray if your objective isn't well defined. Provide your focus with an anchoring object.

Sounds easy enough, doesn't it? Setting objectives can be easy at times. The only objective for the morning is to turn in Report A to the supervisor by 2:00 pm. However, setting a goal can become challenging if you don't have a strict deadline for each item on your incredibly large list

To assist you keep that to-do list structured, come up with a daily routine.

- First, determine your priorities. Put that to-do list in writing. Seeing everything in front of you, whether it's digital or handwritten, is what matters.

- Now that you have your priorities straight, rank them in order of significance.

Prioritize the ones that are most urgent. Prioritizing and doing the most important things first will help you avoid becoming sidetracked by other distractions.

- Make sure that everything you add to your to-do list gets split into small steps. Next, schedule brief intervals of time to concentrate solely on the items on your list. If it helps you stay on task, set a timer.

- Don't overextend yourself. Not that it's making any difference with that two-mile-long list of objectives for the day. Not many long lists are completed. So just set aside a few of those less critical items. When things are more urgent, you can take care of them another day.

Over time, your ability to focus might be seriously harmed by overcommitting or failing to set reasonable goals. Your brain is trained to expect failure when you repeatedly set lofty goals and then fall short of them.

Don't make a two-mile-long list; instead, stick to the things that are most important. Keep in mind that you may always come back and create a fresh list of objectives after completing those top priorities.

Get Rid of Distractions

Distractions must be removed if you want your mind to be ready to concentrate. Modern distractions are complex and contribute significantly to the issue. It might be difficult to focus on the task at hand when there are distractions around your workplace or on your phone.

What could be obstructing your view then? You must recognize it for what it is in order to remove it.

Physical Distractions

Physical distractions are easy to foresee and prepare for in advance. Most of the time, all it takes is following a regular daily schedule. Take the time to foresee issues and find solutions before they interfere with your ability to concentrate.

- Hunger

When you're trying to get things started, do you always realize you're hungry? Never miss breakfast.

You can prepare ahead of time and keep a convenient snack near your workspace, even if you're not the kind to start your day with a meal. Before attempting to begin, eat.

- The temperature

It is difficult to maintain mental attention on a computer screen when you are excessively hot or chilly. Ideally, you will be able to regulate the temperature in your workspace and identify the ideal temperature before you begin. However, in practice, you can have absolutely no control. You still have time to make plans.

Do you work in a consistently chilly workplace setting? Have a lightweight jacket or sweater on hand for when the weather turns chilly. Feel consistently much warmer than your colleagues? Maintain a fan on your desk.

- Sound

Another aspect of the surroundings that you might not always be able to control is noise. Possible causes include obtrusive music coming through the shared wall or phones ringing at adjacent desks. Some people can shut out everything at will, while others are easily distracted by sounds of any kind.

When you need to concentrate on something, think about wearing a pair of noise-canceling headphones if you already know that this is something that distracts you.

Digital Distractions

Our minds are already being reprogrammed to be constantly linked by the modern lifestyle. Digital distractions rank as the biggest problem for a lot of people. But you can also prepare for these interruptions.

- Phones

Put your phone on DND "do not disturb" mode or completely disable the ringer. Put your phone away so it's completely hidden. Taking the phone away will not only keep an unknown caller from interfering with your concentration, but it will also remove the temptation to glance at smartphone app notifications as they come up.

- Email

Shut down your email app entirely. You can't put your emails out of your mind until they're completely out of sight, much like with your phone. You should probably include this on your list of things to do. Therefore, schedule a period just for responding to emails, and feel free to ignore them while working on other tasks.

- Social Media

Social media is made with the express purpose of luring you back again and time again. The platforms use psychological tricks to maintain your interest. Your brain experiences a small dopamine surge each and every time you interact. Social media is one of the biggest drains on your mental focus since it constantly leaves you wanting more.

Examine your preferred social media network, and then log off. If required, disable app notifications for your social media accounts. You might also want to think about making it a practice to avoid using any websites or social media apps during designated times of the day.

Can't begin without resolving every distraction you've encountered online? Make early plans for that as well. Give yourself a deadline to address each of those issues. Next, set a timer. Giving yourself some time to "get it out of your system" will prevent you from thinking about what you might be overlooking online.

Stimulate Your Brain

Research has repeatedly demonstrated what people have understood for ages. There's a connection between coffee and mind. The brain can be awakened and concentration made easier by caffeine. Perhaps all it takes to get things going is reaching for a cup of coffee.

This is one you might want to hold onto for the days when things are a little bit harder for you. However, if drinking tea or coffee in the morning is a regular part of your day, make sure you're not inadvertently missing it. possibly though caffeine "withdraw" is generally minor, it can nevertheless make your brain fog up or possibly give you a terrible headache. These two items won't assist you in maintaining your attention on the current task.

Intolerant to caffeine? Look for additional healthy snacks that will improve your cognitive abilities. Chocolate, avocados, and walnuts are all good sources of brainpower. Each of these has inherent qualities that could aid with concentration.

Naturally, poor food and beverage choices can also deplete your brain's vitality and ability to focus. Treats and sodas with high sugar content should be avoided since they can lead to fluctuations in blood sugar levels. Your energy is depleted as a result, leaving you drowsy or lethargic.

Listen to some background music

This one might seem like it shouldn't work after you have taken such care to minimize physical distractions. Isn't music listening distracting? Of course, it can be a major distraction for some individuals. You should avoid this one if that applies to you. However, studies have indicated that background music—especially instrumental music—can aid in mental concentration.

Are you aware that you are among the few individuals who can be distracted by music, even if it is instrumental? Instead, think about turning on some white noise. Make sure the background music you pick to play is something you love listening to, as it won't likely be of any use otherwise. That's right, you have the right to become irritated when the man next door starts playing loud music when you're trying to get work done.

Take Breaks

You have thus tried every one of these things. After a while, you still notice that your thoughts are wandering even though it is making some progress. It does, of course! The brain is a creature of novelty. Your brain begins searching for something new after extended periods of time spent concentrating on anything. This is where taking a quick pause might help you focus and reenergize your mind.

Do:

- Take a stroll around the workplace or go outdoors to get some fresh air. You can extend your legs and increase blood flow by walking. If you need to use the restroom, grab a food or a drink. If you ignore your body's physical requirements right now, they may become a distraction when you try to resume your work.

Don't:

- Give in to the need to check your emails, voicemails, or app notifications. Digital diversions have the power to totally hijack your time, focus, and vitality.

As with everything else, schedule these breaks in advance to avoid issues developing on their own. Divide your job into manageable "bites" before you begin working on it, and schedule brief breaks in between the sections. By doing this, you will probably discover that your ability to focus on the subject at hand is restored when you return to your work.

Anyone can learn to focus more intently mentally. The most important things are to set up efficient routines and manage your surroundings. You may incorporate these strategies into your everyday routine by using them consistently.

You should also think about making any other lifestyle adjustments that could be necessary to address the issue. It might not be sufficient to only reduce distractions and make your workspaces more comfortable.

It could be really challenging to increase your concentrate if you are not receiving adequate sleep at night. Nowadays, a lot of folks are doing really well if they receive 6-7 hours of sleep every night. Your ability to concentrate can also be greatly impacted by what you eat and how frequently you exercise. That's why maintaining a balanced diet and engaging in regular exercise are the greatest long-term strategies for enhancing mental clarity. To find out if you need to make any changes, be honest with yourself.

Additionally, if your efforts are not producing the desired outcomes, don't be hesitant to ask for assistance. You don't have to handle this by yourself. See a physician or therapist who can assist you in ruling out any more potential causes. You can also feel more certain that you are headed in the right direction by consulting an expert.

Lastly, confirm your belief in your ability to get better. It has been demonstrated that telling oneself repeatedly that you are incapable of improving at anything can lead to a self-fulfilling prophesy. Never let yourself think that it's difficult to break a negative habit. Rather, adopt a "I Can Do It" mentality. The first and most important step in taking charge of your concentration is this. Begin each day with a cheerful outlook, a well-defined plan, and defined expectations.

Conclusion

<u>Conclusion</u>

It's never easy to stay focused in this digital age. Numerous things have the potential to capture our interest, making it simple for us to become sidetracked and lose concentration on the task at hand. We could get a strong impulse to check a notice on social media, a text message, or even an email instead of working on our tasks. Every one of these breaks may cost us productive time that could be used to finish our work.

We looked at how the brain processes attention in this book, and we also went over some of the various strategies and tactics you may employ to help yourself become more focused. This is not a procedure that will be completed quickly. It can be difficult to resist the urge to check your email or look at your phone one more time when you are easily distracted. However, by gradually putting some of the concepts and methods in this manual into practice, you can gradually sharpen your attention and regain control over your schedule.

If you found this Book to be helpful and enjoyable, please consider leaving a review! It's a sign of appreciation.

THE FOCUS JOURNAL

FOCUS JOURNAL

MONTH:

EVERYDAY TASK

MON

TUE

WED

THU

FRI

SAT

TOP PRIORITY

CHECKLIST

HABITS

S M T W T F S

BRAIN DUMP

FOCUS JOURNAL

MONTH:

EVERYDAY TASK

MON

TUE.

WED

THU

FRI

SAT

TOP PRIORITY

CHECKLIST

HABITS

S M T W T F S

BRAIN DUMP

FOCUS JOURNAL

MONTH:

EVERYDAY TASK

MON

TUE

WED

THU

FRI

SAT

TOP PRIORITY

CHECKLIST

HABITS

S M T W T F S

BRAIN DUMP

FOCUS JOURNAL

MONTH : _______________

EVERYDAY TASK

MON

TUE

WED

THU

FRI

SAT

TOP PRIORITY

CHECKLIST

HABITS

S M T W T F S

BRAIN DUMP

FOCUS JOURNAL

MONTH :

EVERYDAY TASK

MON

TUE

WED

THU

FRI

SAT

TOP PRIORITY

CHECKLIST

HABITS

S M T W T F S

BRAIN DUMP

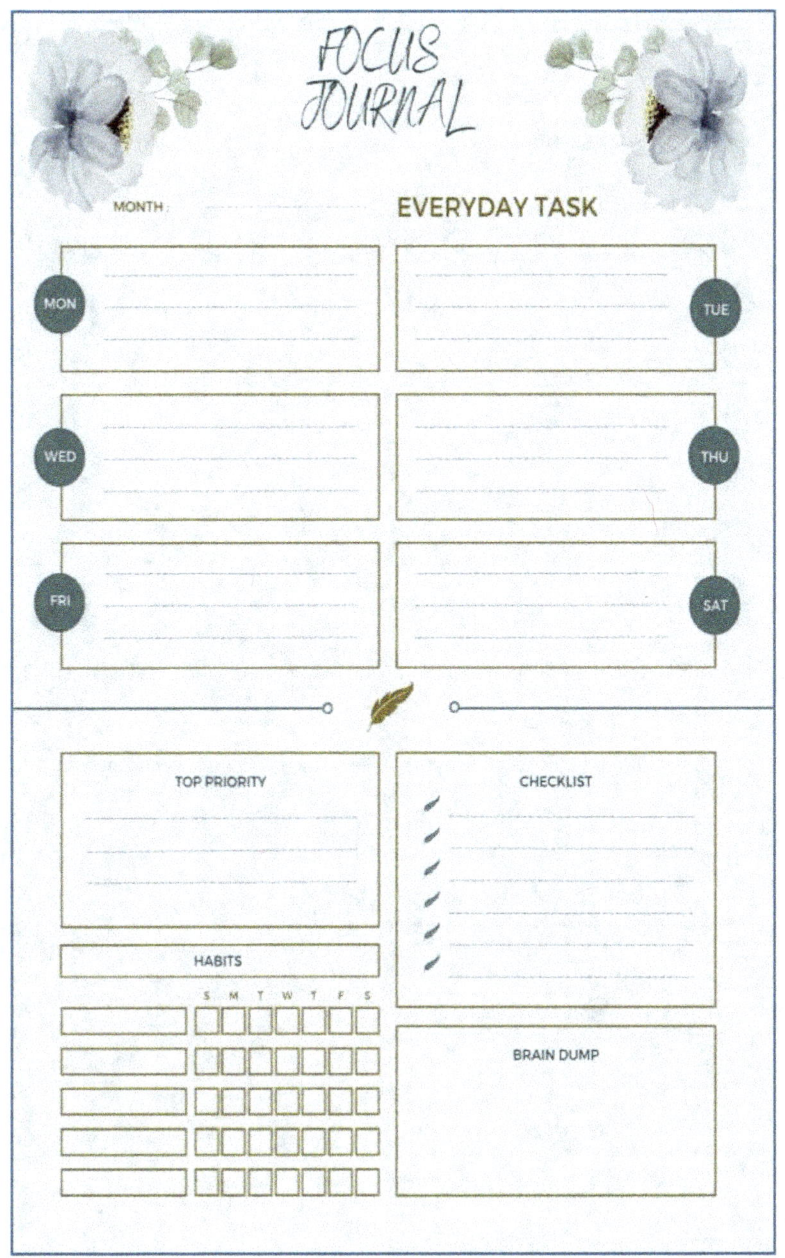

FOCUS JOURNAL

MONTH :

EVERYDAY TASK

MON
TUE
WED
THU
FRI
SAT

TOP PRIORITY

CHECKLIST

HABITS
S M T W T F S

BRAIN DUMP

FOCUS JOURNAL

MONTH: ___________________

EVERYDAY TASK

MON

TUE

WED

THU

FRI

SAT

TOP PRIORITY

HABITS

S M T W T F S

CHECKLIST

BRAIN DUMP

FOCUS JOURNAL

MONTH:

EVERYDAY TASK

MON

TUE

WED

THU

FRI

SAT

TOP PRIORITY

HABITS

S M T W T F S

CHECKLIST

BRAIN DUMP

FOCUS JOURNAL

MONTH:

EVERYDAY TASK

MON

TUE

WED

THU

FRI

SAT

TOP PRIORITY

CHECKLIST

HABITS

S M T W T F S

BRAIN DUMP

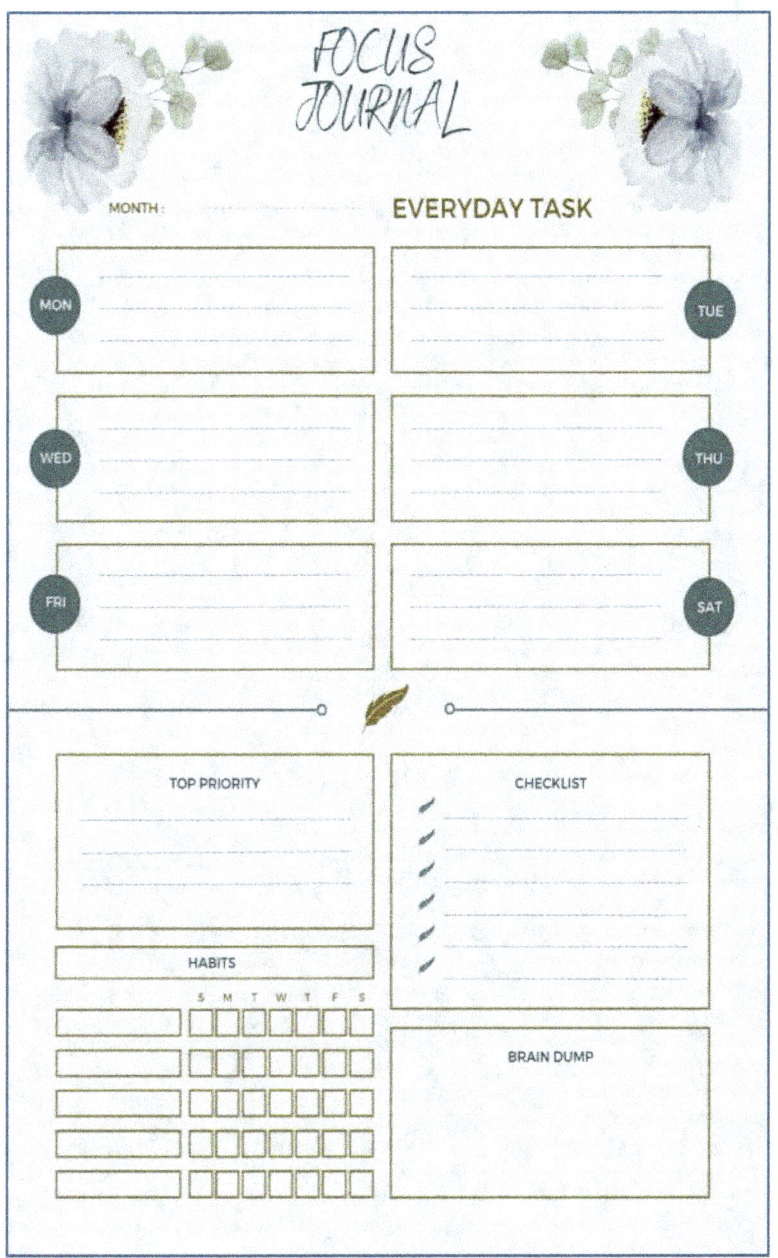
FOCUS JOURNAL

MONTH :

EVERYDAY TASK

MON
TUE
WED
THU
FRI
SAT

TOP PRIORITY

CHECKLIST

HABITS

S M T W T F S

BRAIN DUMP

FOCUS JOURNAL

MONTH :

EVERYDAY TASK

MON

TUE

WED

THU

FRI

SAT

TOP PRIORITY

CHECKLIST

HABITS

S M T W T F S

BRAIN DUMP

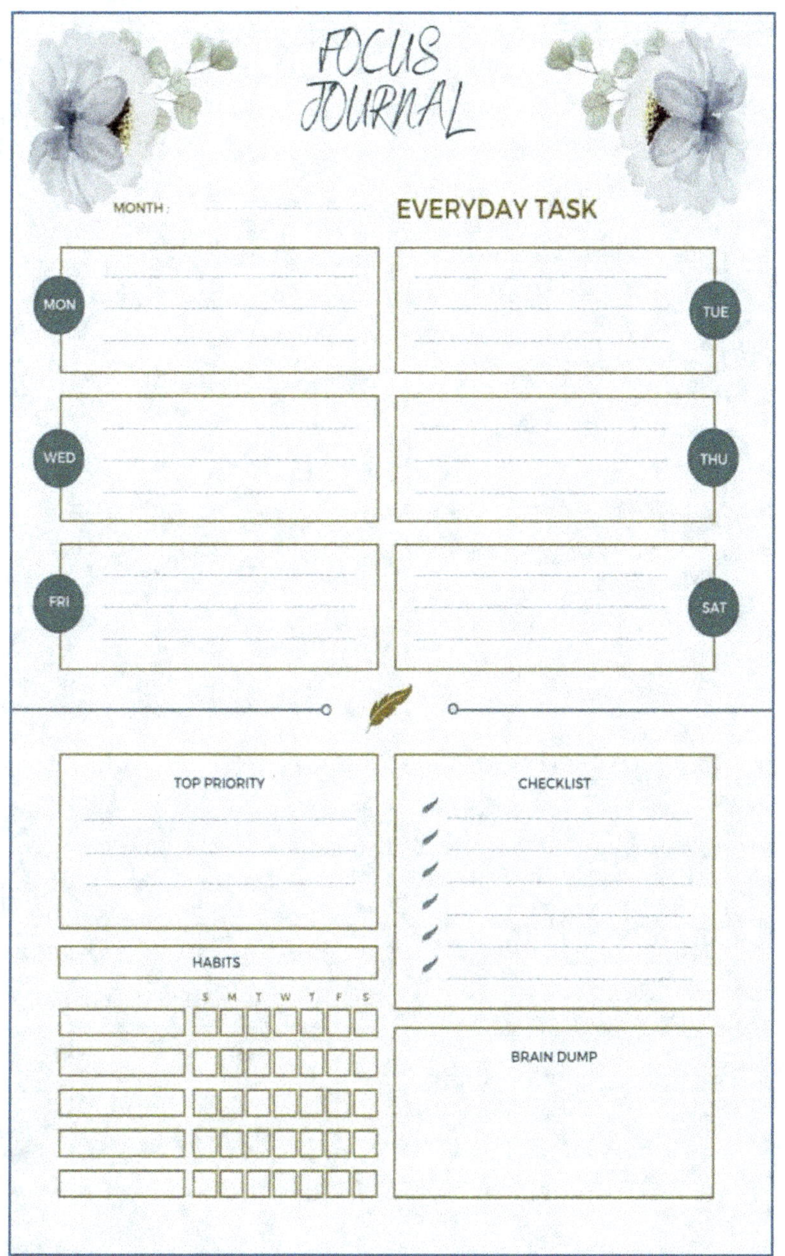
FOCUS JOURNAL
MONTH :
EVERYDAY TASK
MON
TUE
WED
THU
FRI
SAT
TOP PRIORITY
CHECKLIST
HABITS
S M T W T F S
BRAIN DUMP

FOCUS JOURNAL

MONTH :

EVERYDAY TASK

MON

TUE

WED

THU

FRI

SAT

TOP PRIORITY

CHECKLIST

HABITS

S M T W T F S

BRAIN DUMP

FOCUS JOURNAL

MONTH :

EVERYDAY TASK

MON

TUE

WED

THU

FRI

SAT

TOP PRIORITY

CHECKLIST

HABITS

S M T W T F S

BRAIN DUMP

FOCUS JOURNAL

MONTH :

EVERYDAY TASK

MON

TUE

WED

THU

FRI

SAT

TOP PRIORITY

CHECKLIST

HABITS

S M T W T F S

BRAIN DUMP

FOCUS JOURNAL

MONTH :

EVERYDAY TASK

MON

TUE

WED

THU

FRI

SAT

TOP PRIORITY

CHECKLIST

HABITS

S M T W T F S

BRAIN DUMP

MONTH :

EVERYDAY TASK

MON

TUE

WED

THU

FRI

SAT

TOP PRIORITY

CHECKLIST

HABITS

S M T W T F S

BRAIN DUMP

FOCUS JOURNAL

MONTH :

EVERYDAY TASK

MON

TUE

WED

THU

FRI

SAT

TOP PRIORITY

CHECKLIST

HABITS

S M T W T F S

BRAIN DUMP

MONTH :

EVERYDAY TASK

MON

TUE

WED

THU

FRI

SAT

TOP PRIORITY

CHECKLIST

HABITS

S M T W T F S

BRAIN DUMP

MONTH :

EVERYDAY TASK

MON

TUE

WED

THU

FRI

SAT

TOP PRIORITY

CHECKLIST

HABITS

S M T W T F S

BRAIN DUMP

MONTH :

EVERYDAY TASK

MON

TUE

WED

THU

FRI

SAT

TOP PRIORITY

CHECKLIST

HABITS

S M T W T F S

BRAIN DUMP

FOCUS JOURNAL

MONTH : _______________

EVERYDAY TASK

MON

TUE

WED

THU

FRI

SAT

TOP PRIORITY

CHECKLIST

HABITS

S M T W T F S

BRAIN DUMP